NATIVE
AMERICANS

ALGONQUIN

Big Buddy Books
An Imprint of Abdo Publishing
www.abdopublishing.com

Sarah Tieck

www.abdopublishing.com

Published by Abdo Publishing, a division of ABDO, PO Box 398166, Minneapolis, Minnesota 55439.
Copyright © 2015 by Abdo Consulting Group, Inc. International copyrights reserved in all countries. No part
of this book may be reproduced in any form without written permission from the publisher. Big Buddy Books™
is a trademark and logo of Abdo Publishing.

Printed in the United States of America, North Mankato, Minnesota.
042014
092014

Cover Photo: © Francis Vachon/Alamy.
Interior Photos: © Hemis/Alamy (p. 25); iStockphoto (p. 11); © NativeStock.com/AngelWynn (pp. 9, 13, 15, 17, 23,
     27, 29); © Martin Paquin/Alamy (p. 30); Shutterstock (pp. 19, 21, 26); UIG via Getty Images (pp. 5, 16).

Coordinating Series Editor: Rochelle Baltzer
Contributing Editors: Bridget O'Brien, Marcia Zappa
Graphic Design: Adam Craven

Library of Congress Cataloging-in-Publication Data

Tieck, Sarah, 1976-
  Algonquin / Sarah Tieck.
     pages cm -- (Native Americans)
  ISBN 978-1-62403-350-6
1. Algonquin Indians--Juvenile literature. I. Title.
  E99.A349T54 2015
  973.04'973--dc23
                           2014005025

CONTENTS

Amazing People 4

Algonquin Territory 6

Home Life 8

What They Ate 10

Daily Life 14

Made by Hand 16

Spirit Life 18

Storytellers 20

Fighting for Land 22

Back in Time 26

A Strong Nation 28

Glossary 31

Websites 31

Index 32

Amazing People

Hundreds of years ago, North America was mostly wild, open land. Native Americans lived on the land. They had their own languages and **customs**.

The Algonquin (al-GAHN-kwuhn) are one Native American nation. They are known for their smart traders and hard workers. Let's learn more about this Native American nation and its way of life.

No one is sure exactly where the Algonquin got their name. But, it is believed the word might be close to a Maliseet word. That word means "they are our allies."

ALGONQUIN TERRITORY

There are many bands of Algonquin. The Algonquin homelands were in present-day Quebec and Ontario, Canada.

The tribe lived in thick forests near the Ottawa River. The people hunted and gathered food from the land. They used water from rivers for daily life. And, they used parts of trees to build homes and tools.

Did You Know?

In Canada, many Native Americans are called First Nations people.

CANADA

ALGONQUIN HOMELANDS

QUEBEC

CANADA

ONTARIO

UNITED STATES

UNITED STATES

MEXICO

HOME LIFE

The Algonquin lived in groups of 100 to 300 people. When winter moved in, they split into smaller groups.

The people lived in homes called wigwams. These were made of strong sticks bent into an upside-down "U" shape. They were covered with woven grasses or tree bark. These homes were strong, but easy to build.

Did You Know?

Parents, children, and even grown children often lived together.

A wigwam was about 15 to 20 feet (4.6 to 6.1 m) across.

What They Ate

The Algonquin gathered wild plants, including berries, nuts, and roots. Sometimes tribes traded with each other for food, such as corn.

The Algonquin did a small amount of farming. Some people tapped maple trees for sap. When winter came, they moved around to find food.

Did You Know?

Algonquins traded objects such as beaver pelts or furs. In return, other tribes, such as the Huron, gave them corn.

During late winter and early spring, sweet-water sap flows out of holes cut in sugar maple trees. It can be made into syrup.

In addition to gathering food, the Algonquin hunted animals and caught fish. They made spears and bows and arrows to hunt deer and moose. They used canoes for fishing in lakes and rivers.

Did You Know?

Algonquins are known for their canoes. These were an important way to travel in spring, summer, and fall. In winter, they used toboggans and snowshoes.

Have you ever been fishing? The Algonquin didn't use modern fishing poles with hooks. Instead, they would often stick fish with spears.

Daily Life

In each Algonquin band, people had different jobs. Men were warriors and hunters. Some were chiefs. Women gathered food, cooked meals, and took care of the children. Men and women told stories and made art.

The children helped their parents. They played with toys that prepared them for adult life. Dolls were often attached to cradleboards, much like Algonquin babies in real life.

The Algonquin cooked using clay pots. They roasted foods over the fire on sticks called spits.

MADE BY HAND

The Algonquin made their clothes, tools, and other objects by hand. Their arts and crafts added beauty to everyday life. But, they also had important uses.

Beaded Clothes
The Algonquin made headbands, dresses, cloaks, and leggings. They often decorated their clothes with beautiful beads and patterns.

Artful Baskets

Algonquin baskets were works of art. People made beautiful patterns on birchbark. The baskets were used for collecting food.

Wampum Belts

Algonquins wove belts using white and purple shell beads. The shapes and pictures told stories.

Birchbark Canoes

The Algonquin are known for their canoes. To make one, they stretched birchbark over a wooden frame.

17

Spirit Life

Religion was important to the Algonquin way of life. They believed the most powerful god was the Great Spirit. They believed that there were other good and evil spirits in the world. Shamans were spiritual advisors to the tribe.

Tribe members paid attention to their dreams. They thought these had messages for them. They also took part in **ceremonies** to honor spirits.

During a smudging ceremony, people burned sacred plants. They used the smoke to clean themselves before a spiritual gathering.

STORYTELLERS

The Algonquin told stories. These folktales and myths taught people history and lessons. Some stories were told just for fun! Storytelling was a way to pass on ideas and beliefs to new **generations**. It was also a way to share stories about families.

Many Algonquin stories are about the earth. For example, one tells how it was created.

FIGHTING FOR LAND

The Algonquin were a strong tribe. In the 1600s, they traded and made friends with the Huron tribe and French settlers.

The Iroquois (IHR-uh-kwoy) were an enemy group. They fought against the Algonquin, the Huron, and the French over land and for power. The Algonquin lost their fight and much of their land. Many died from European sicknesses, such as **smallpox**.

The Algonquin hunted beavers. Then, they traded the furs with the Huron and French settlers.

23

Modern Algonquins work to **protect** their land. In the 1980s, they stood up to companies trying to take wild rice from their land. They **blockaded** areas to stop the companies.

In 2000, the Algonquin helped stop a mine from becoming a garbage dump. And in 2007, they worked to stop **sacred** land from being mined. The tribe wanted to save their land and its **resources**.

Over the years, Algonquins have stopped companies trying to take wood from their land.

BACK IN TIME

1632

The Algonquin were first mentioned in *The Jesuit Relations*. These papers describe religious missions.

1603

Samuel de Champlain of France explored the Saint Lawrence River area. There, he met some Algonquins.

Mid-1600s

Thousands of Algonquins died from **smallpox**.

1981

An Algonquin tribe tried to stop a business from taking wild rice from their land. They blocked roads and spoke out for 27 days. The government stopped the business.

2014

There are more than 5,000 people of Algonquin descent. There are nine groups in Quebec and one in Ontario.

1853

The largest Algonquin **reserve** was started. It was called Kitigan Zibi.

A Strong Nation

The Algonquin people have a long, rich history. They are remembered for their wigwams and birchbark canoes. They are known for their strong people.

Algonquin roots run deep. Today, the people have kept alive those special things that make them Algonquin. Even though times have changed, many people carry the **traditions**, stories, and memories of the past into the present.

Algonquin people gather for powwows.
This is one way of sharing their traditions.

"I would very much like to see whoever created us, who made us to be in this world, understand us and help us to gain the right way. Because we can't do it alone. You need to act together."

— William Commanda

GLOSSARY

blockade to stop people or supplies from entering or leaving an area.

ceremony a formal event on a special occasion.

custom a practice that has been around a long time and is common to a group or a place.

generation (jeh-nuh-RAY-shuhn) a single step in the history of a family.

protect (pruh-TEHKT) to guard against harm or danger.

reserve a piece of land set aside by the government for Native Americans to live on.

resource a supply of something useful or valued.

sacred (SAY-kruhd) connected with worship of a god.

smallpox a sickness that causes fever, skin marks, and often death.

tradition (truh-DIH-shuhn) a belief, a custom, or a story handed down from older people to younger people.

WEBSITES

To learn more about Native Americans, visit **booklinks.abdopublishing.com**. These links are routinely monitored and updated to provide the most current information available.

INDEX

arts and crafts **14, 16, 17**

Canada **6, 27**

canoes **12, 17, 28**

Champlain, Samuel de **26**

clothing **16**

Commanda, William **30**

farming **10**

fishing **12, 13**

food **6, 10, 11, 12, 14, 15, 17, 24, 27**

France **22, 23, 26**

homelands **6, 22, 24, 25, 27**

hunting **6, 12, 14, 23**

Huron **10, 22, 23**

Iroquois **22**

Jesuit Relations, The **26**

Kitigan Zibi **27**

language **4**

Maliseet **5**

Ottawa River **6**

religion **18, 19**

Saint Lawrence River **26**

stories **14, 17, 20, 21, 28**

trading **4, 10, 22, 23**

wigwams **8, 9, 28**